Praise for The Too Tall Giraffe

It was great!

—Savannah, Age 8

The giraffe is so adorable.

—Clara, Age 8

I loved it! 10/10!!! My favorite part was the picture of the lion with all the teeth.

—Emerson, Age 5

The Too Tall Giraffe is a fun story! I liked the part about trying to reach the leaves, so they stuck their tongues out farther. That was funny. I think this is a very good book. I think it's good to know that even if you look different, you can still do good and help people.

—Harrison, Age 10

Published by Author Academy Elite
PO Box 43, Powell, OH 43065

Identifiers:

Library of Congress Control Number: 2021901732
Paperback: 978-1-64746-705-0
Hardcover: 978-1-64746-706-7
E-book: 978-1-64746-707-4

Available in paperback, hardback, and E-book
TheChristineMaier.com

The Too Tall Giraffe

A Children's Book about Looking Different,
Fitting in, and Finding Your Superpower

By Christine Maier
Illustrated by Aviva Brueckner

Dedication

Max, Lucas, Alex, and Matt

Always be different!

Savannah whistled goodbye to her brother, Forrest, and paced to school with her mom and dad.

When Savannah reached the classroom, she smiled down on her new classmates, Henry, Dawn, and Addison. They didn't smile back. Instead, they whispered about her.

"Did you see how tall she is?"

"Giraffe calves aren't that tall."

"Do you think Mrs. Branch is tricking us?"

Mom brought a stool to help Forrest climb onto Savannah's back. She once again felt sad she was too tall and didn't want to play anymore.

"I'm tired. Better go do my homework."

"Can we play later?"

One day while walking to school, Savannah observed something lurking in the grass. She asked the other giraffes if they had seen it, but they weren't tall enough to see over the fence.

A noise from outside the yard interrupted the eating giraffes. Savannah looked over the fence and saw the scariest lion *ever*.

Even though she was scared, Savannah remembered Mrs. Branch's lesson about lions. She let out the loudest snort she could muster to alert the other giraffes of the danger. When they saw how scared she was, they galloped away.

Savannah galloped home as fast as she could,
worried she hadn't snorted right.

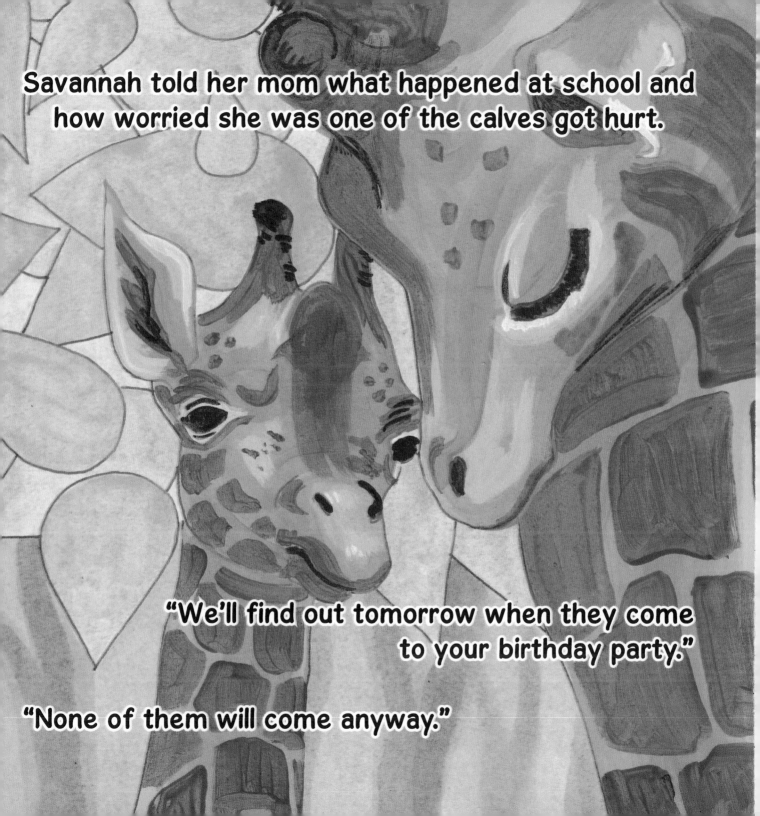

Savannah told her mom what happened at school and how worried she was one of the calves got hurt.

"We'll find out tomorrow when they come to your birthday party."

"None of them will come anyway."

The next day, Savannah turned four. She prepared to spend the day with her family, worried about her classmates. But one by one, the calves from her class showed up at her house for the party.

"Thanks for saving us from the lions yesterday."

"We're lucky you're so tall and could see the lions."

"Happy Birthday, Savannah!"

Christine Maier

Christine Maier is an author, coach, and speaker helping individuals and organizations turn obstacles into opportunities to understand their beauty, purpose, and power.

Christine spent years believing a cleft lip and palate, being the shortest kid in class, and a learning disability were holding her back. But the opposite was true. They taught her that what makes us different is really the foundation for understanding our superpowers.

Aviva Brueckner

Aviva Brueckner is a writer and artist heavily influenced by her front-row seat to peaceful revolution. Born to an Israeli mother and a German father in East-Berlin, she joined the street protests rattling her country at age 13 and toppled the Wall.

Avi has degrees in law, physical therapy, and graphic design. She has lived in three countries on three continents and has traveled many more, usually on a shoestring budget. Proud Aspie.

A child is born worldwide with a cleft every 3 minutes.

Christine Maier was born with a cleft lip and palate and had over 25 surgeries; her first at four months old. Christine not only looked different growing up, she struggled with her speech, and too often, missed school for surgeries and treatments. A learning disability added to her challenges and her small size made her a last round pick in the elementary school kickball draft.

As an International speaker and author, Christine helps children and adults understand that not only is different cool, it is also the foundation of our superpowers. Christine is a member of the Cleft Community Advisory Council (CCAC) for Smile Train and a member of the Children's Craniofacial Association Speakers' Bureau.

Learn more at
TheChristineMaier.com

children's craniofacial association
www.ccakids.org

The mission of the Children's Craniofacial Association (CCA) is to empower and give hope to individuals and families affected by facial differences. CCA assists with medical, financial, psychosocial, emotional, and educational concerns relating to craniofacial conditions.

Free resources from CCA are available to parents and teachers about craniofacial conditions. The #ChooseKind Initiative aims to develop kindness education and prevent bullying, intolerance, and isolation that so many children face at school each day.

The Children's Craniofacial Association Speakers' Bureau provides a positive platform to talk about differences confidently. Teachers report it is incredibly impactful when students use the Children's Craniofacial Association books and experience their presentations.

Learn more at CCAKIDS.org

SPEAKERS' BUREAU
CHILDREN'S CRANIOFACIAL ASSOCIATION